Samsung Galax Manual for Beginners and Seniors

The Ultimate User Guide to Master Your New Smartphone as a Professional

Helen Smiler

Table of Contents

Introduction

Controlling the full potential of your Samsung Galaxy A16 with this comprehensive, easy-to-follow guide! Whether you're a beginner setting up your first smartphone or a tech-savvy user looking to explore advanced features, this book provides everything you need to get the most out of your device.

Inside, you'll discover:

- ✓ Step-by-step setup instructions for seamless activation
- ✓ Expert tips on navigation, customization, and essential settings
- ✓ Advanced camera techniques for stunning photos and videos
- ✓ Battery optimization strategies to extend usage time
- ✓ Security features like facial recognition, fingerprint scanning, and Samsung Pass
- ✓ Productivity hacks, multi-window multitasking, and time-saving gestures
- ✓ Troubleshooting solutions for common issues

With clear explanations and illustrated tutorials, this guide transforms the Samsung Galaxy A16 into your ultimate tool for communication, entertainment, and productivity. Whether you're switching from another phone or upgrading to the latest Galaxy model, this book ensures you maximize every feature and function.

📖 **Get your copy today and master your Samsung Galaxy A16 with confidence!**

Chapter One
Get to Know Your Device

What's in the Box, Key Features, and First Impressions

Unboxing the Samsung Galaxy A16

When you open your Samsung Galaxy A16 box, you'll typically find the following items:

- Samsung Galaxy A16 smartphone
- USB-C charging cable
- Wall adapter (charger)
- SIM ejector tool
- Quick start guide
- Warranty card

First Impressions

The Galaxy A16 is designed with simplicity and style in mind, making it ideal for both beginners and seniors. It is well equipped with sleek plastic body, a comfortable grip, a large and vibrant display that's easy on the eyes.

Right out of the box, you'll notice

- A large display that's great for reading, videos, and browsing.
- A clean layout with minimal buttons for easy navigation.

Key Physical Features

Here's a quick overview of the physical components:

- **Front:**
  - Large touchscreen display
- Front-facing camera
- **Back:**
  - Main camera(s) and flash
  - Samsung logo
- **Sides:**
  - Power button (may also function as a fingerprint scanner)
  - Volume up/down buttons
- **Bottom:**
  - USB-C charging port
  - Speaker
  - Headphone jack (if included in your model)

Key Features of the Galaxy A16

- 6.5" HD+ Display – Bright and sharp for everything from reading to streaming.

- Long-Lasting Battery – Designed to get you through the day on a single charge.

- Multi-Camera System – Capture great photos with various lenses.

- Expandable Storage – Add a microSD card to store more apps, photos, and videos.

- Security Features – Fingerprint scanner and face unlock for easy access.

Why It's Great for Beginners and Seniors

- Easy Setup with step-by-step guidance.

- Accessible Mode for simplified controls.

- Voice Commands via Google Assistant.

Chapter Two
Getting Started

Setting Up Your Phone, Inserting SIM/microSD, Charging, and Initial Configuration

1. Charging Your Phone

Before anything else, give your Galaxy A16 a full charge to ensure smooth setup.

- **Step 1:** Carefully connect the USB-C cable into the charging adapter.
- **Step 2:** You can also plug the adapter to a power outlet.
- **Step 3:** At the bottom of the phone simply place the USB-C end into the charging port.

Tip: You can use the phone while it charges, but a full first charge is recommended.

2. Inserting the SIM Card and microSD Card

To make calls, use mobile data, or expand your storage, you'll need to insert a SIM card and optionally a microSD card.

What You Need:

- The SIM ejector tool (included in the box)
- Your SIM card (nano SIM)
- Optional: microSD card (for extra storage)

Steps:

1. Locate the SIM tray on the left side of your phone.
2. Place the SIM ejector tool into the little hole close to the tray.
3. The tray will pop out. Gently pull it out.
4. Place the nano SIM in the SIM slot (label side up).
5. If using a microSD card, insert it into the designated slot.
6. Push the tray back in until it clicks to the original place.

To avoid damage, please make sure the cards are properly aligned.

3. Powering On the Device

- Press and hold the Power button (on the right side of the phone) for a few seconds until the Samsung logo appears.

- Wait for the phone to boot up. This usually takes a minute or two on the first run.

4. Initial Configuration (Setup Wizard)

Once powered on, you'll be guided through Samsung's easy Setup Wizard. Here's what you'll do:

A. Select Your Language and Region

Choose your preferred language and country/region.

B. Connect to Wi-Fi

- Select the Wi-Fi network and type in your password.

- Or, you can skip and use mobile data (if SIM is inserted).

C. Sign in to Google Account

- You can simply login with your Google account to go in Gmail, Google Play Store, and many more.

- You can do it later if preferred by skipping.

D. Accept Terms and Conditions

- You can review and simply agree to Samsung's and Google's terms.

E. Set Up a Screen Lock

- Choose a screen lock method: pattern, PIN, password, fingerprint, or face recognition.
- This keeps your device secure.

F. Samsung Account (Optional but Recommended)

- Sign in or create a Samsung account to access Samsung services like SmartThings, Samsung Cloud, and Galaxy Store.

5. Finishing Touches

- Choose your preferred font size and display zoom.
- Enable/disable Google Assistant and location services.
- You can simply explore the home screen after the setup is completed.

Chapter Three
Navigating the Interface

Understanding the Home Screen, Navigation Buttons, Status Bar, and Gestures

1. The Home Screen at a Glance

When you turn on your Galaxy A16, the first thing you'll see is the home screen – your main dashboard for apps, widgets, and shortcuts.

Key Parts of the Home Screen

- App Icons: These are shortcuts to open your favorite apps like Phone, Messages, Camera, and more.

- Dock (Bottom Row): Fixed apps that stay visible on every home screen page (usually includes Phone, Messages, Internet, and Camera).

- Widgets: Small panels that show info like weather, calendar, or clock.

- Pages: Swipe left or right to access additional screens for more apps.

- Google Search Bar: Quickly search the web or your device.

You can simply customize this screen with the applications and widgets you use often.

2. Navigation Buttons (or Gestures)

Depending on your settings, you'll use either navigation buttons or swipe gestures to move around your phone.

Navigation Buttons (default for beginners)

- Back Button (◀): Takes you one step back in any app or screen.

- Home Button (●): Simply brings you back to the home screen from anywhere.

- Recent Apps Button (≡ or ▢): Shows apps you've recently used so you can quickly switch or close them.

Normally these buttons are usually located at the bottom of the screen.

3. The Status Bar (Top of Screen)

The status bar runs across the top of your screen and shows quick info at a glance:

- Time
- Battery level
- Signal strength
- Wi-Fi or Mobile Data status
- Bluetooth, Alarm, Do Not Disturb, etc.

Swipe Down to Reveal the Notification Panel

- See missed calls, messages, app alerts.
- Access Quick Settings like Wi-Fi, Sound, Flashlight, Airplane Mode.

You can customize what appears here too!

4. Tips for Smooth Navigation

- Pinch with your two fingers on the home screen to access edit mode.
- To change or delete it hold and drag an application.
- Tap and hold on an empty area to change wallpaper or add widgets.

Common Icons You'll See

Icon	Meaning
	Signal strength (mobile network)
	Battery level
	Vibrate or silent mode
	Screen is locked
	Notification alerts
	Wi-Fi connected
	Airplane mode enabled

You're now familiar with the layout and how to get around with ease!

Chapter Four
Customizing Your Phone

Themes, Wallpapers, Widgets, Fonts, and Display Settings to Make It Yours

1. Changing Wallpapers

Wallpapers set the mood of your phone.

How to Change Your Wallpaper

1. You can long press on an empty space on the home screen (touch and hold).

2. Tap "Wallpapers and style".

3. Choose from My Wallpapers, Gallery, or download more via Galaxy Themes.

4. Tap Set as wallpaper, then choose:

o Home screen

o Lock screen

o Both

You can even use your favorite family photo or pet picture!

2. Applying Themes (Make It Match Your Style)

On your device or smartphone Themes can automatically change the look of icons, colors, and even sounds.

How to Browse and Apply a Theme

1. Navigate to the Settings > Themes or open the Galaxy Themes app.

2. Browse free or paid themes.

3. Tap on one you like, then press Download and Apply.

Themes are very good for creating and making your smartphone fun, seasonal, or elegant.

3. Adding and Using Widgets

Widgets display live information on your home screen — something like weather, calendar, clock, or music controls.

How to Add a Widget

1. Long press on the home screen.

2. Tap Widgets.

3. Browse or search (e.g., Clock, Calendar, Weather).

4. Press and hold down your selected widget, then simply drag it onto your home screen.

To Remove a Widget

- Press and hold it down, then touch Remove.

Widgets are handy for quick info without opening apps.

4. Changing Fonts and Font Size

Make text easier to read with different fonts or larger sizes.

Change Font Style and Size

1. Go down to the Settings > Display > Font size and style.

2. Adjust the Font size slider to make your text larger or smaller.

3. Tap Font style to choose a new look (you can download more fonts too).

5. Adjusting Display Settings

Your screen can adapt to your needs — from brightness to screen timeout.

Key Settings to Explore

- Brightness:
- o Navigate to the Settings > Display
- o Adjust manually or turn on Adaptive brightness to let your phone adjust it automatically.

- **Dark Mode:**

o Easier on the eyes, especially at night.

o Turn it on under Settings > Display > Dark mode.

- **Screen Timeout:**
  - o Set how long the screen stays on before going dark.

o   Adjust under Settings > Display > Screen timeout (e.g., 1 minute, 5 minutes).

- **Screen Zoom:**

  o   In Display > Screen zoom, increase or decrease how large content appears.

All these features help reduce eye strain and make the screen comfortable for daily use.

6. Quick Personalization Tips

- You can simply group applications into folders by dragging one icon over another.
- Rename folders for easy navigation (e.g., "Games", "Health", "Family").

Chapter Five
Essential Settings & Controls

Sound, Notifications, Brightness, Battery, and Accessibility Features

1. Managing Sounds and Volume

Your Galaxy A16 lets you control sounds for calls, media, notifications, and alarms.

Adjusting Volume

1. On the side of the smartphone, you can basically press down the volume buttons.

2. To see or view all volume sliders, you can touch the three dots on the screen:

   o Ringtone

   o Media

   o Notifications

   o System sounds

Silent and Vibrate Mode

- Swipe down to open the Quick Panel, then tap the Sound/Vibrate/Mute icon.

- Locate the Settings > Sounds and vibration to switch modes.

Customize your ringtone and notification sounds from here too.

2. Managing Notifications

Notifications keep you informed, but you can control which ones you see (and hear).

View and Clear Notifications

- From the up of the screen swipe downward.

- To remove or clear them all simply click on the "Clear all" button.

Customize Notifications

1. Navigate to the Settings > Notifications.

2. Choose an app (like Messages or Facebook).

3. Turn notifications on or off, or fine-tune what kind you receive.

You can silence apps that bug you too often without missing the important stuff.

3. Brightness and Display Comfort

A bright screen helps outdoors, but lower brightness saves battery and eases eye strain.

Adjust Brightness

- Swipe down twice and move the brightness slider.

- Locate the Settings > Display > Brightness.

4. Checking and Managing Battery Life

Knowing how your battery is doing helps you avoid running out unexpectedly.

Battery Usage

- Navigate to the Settings > Battery and device care > Battery.

- View which applications that use the most power.

Battery Saver Mode

- Prolong battery life when it's getting low.
- Turn it on under Settings > Battery > Power saving mode.

Tips to Save Battery

- Lower screen brightness
- Turn off Wi-Fi or Bluetooth when not in use
- Close unused apps in the background

5. Accessibility Features (Designed for Ease of Use)

Samsung includes helpful tools for users with vision, hearing, or dexterity needs.

Find These Settings

Navigate to the Settings > Accessibility.

Useful Options

- Visibility Enhancements:
  o Larger fonts
  o High contrast mode
  o Magnifier window
- Hearing Enhancements:

- o Subtitles

- o Sound detectors (for alarms, baby crying)

- • Interaction and Dexterity:

- o Assistant menu for easier tapping

- o Touch and hold delay adjustments

These tools help make the phone more comfortable and usable for everyone.

Chapter Six

Managing Contacts and Calls

Adding, Importing, and Organizing Contacts; Making and Receiving Calls

1. Adding New Contacts

Let's start with saving phone numbers so you can easily call friends, family, or doctors.

How to Add a Contact

1. Open the Phone app (green icon).

2. Tap the Contacts tab.

3. Tap the Add or + icon.

4. Fill in the name, phone number, and other info (email, address, etc.).

5. Tap Save.

Choose where to save: on your phone, SIM card, or Google account. Saving to Google means your contacts are backed up!

2. Importing Contacts from Your Old Phone or SIM Card

If or when you're upgrading from an old telephone or bringing over your SIM:

Import from SIM

1. Navigate to the Contacts > Menu (three lines or dots) > Manage contacts.

2. Tap on the Import or Export contacts > Import.

3. Pick your SIM card and simply select the contacts you desire to copy.

Import from Another Phone

You can use Samsung Smart Switch to transfer everything:

1. Download Smart Switch from the Play Store (if not already installed).

2. Follow the on-screen steps to transfer via cable or wireless.

This brings over not just contacts but also photos, apps, and messages if you want!

3. Organizing Contacts

Keep your contacts neat so it's easy to find who you're looking for.

Create a Group

1. Open Contacts.

2. Tap Groups > Add group.

3. Name your group (e.g., "Family", "Doctors") and add contacts.

Favorite Contacts

- To mark as a favorite simply launch a contact and touch the star icon.

- Favorites show at the top of your contact list for easy access.

Grouping helps especially when you want to send group messages or quickly find close contacts.

4. Making a Call

Once your contacts are saved, calling is super simple.

Call from Contacts

1. Open the Phone app.

2. Tap Contacts, then choose a person.

3. Tap the Phone icon to call.

Dial Manually

1. Tap the Keypad tab in the Phone app.

2. Enter the number and tap Call.

Voice Commands (Optional)

- Use Bixby or Google Assistant:

- "Hey Google, call Sarah."

Voice commands are great if you have trouble seeing small text.

To Answer

- Swipe up or tap Answer (green icon).

To Decline

- Swipe down or tap Decline (red icon).

Options While on a Call

- Speaker: Use hands-free mode.

- Mute: Silence your mic.

6. Blocking Unwanted Calls

Stop spam or robocalls easily.

Chapter Seven
Messaging and Texting

SMS, MMS, and Using Apps Like Samsung Messages or Google Messages

1. What's the Difference?

Let's start by understanding the basics:

- SMS (Short Message Service)
- MMS (Multimedia Messaging Service)

Messages that include pictures, videos, emojis, or long text. Requires mobile data.

- Chat Features (RCS)

Advanced messaging (like iMessage or WhatsApp) through internet or Wi-Fi—shows when someone is typing, sends high-res photos, etc.

Your Galaxy A16 can do all of these depending on your messaging app and carrier support.

2. Choosing a Messaging App

Your phone likely has two options:

- Samsung Messages – The default on the Samsung Smartphones
- Google Messages – Another free, powerful texting app

Both are great! If you want Google Messages

- Navigate to the Play Store, search for Google Messages, and install.
- Set it as your default if prompted.

3. Sending a Basic Text (SMS)

Let's send a simple message!

1. Open your preferred Messages app.
2. Tap the + icon or Start Chat.
3. Input the contact or number of the person you desire to message.
4. In the text box compose your message.
5. Tap Send (paper airplane icon).

That's it—you just sent a text!

4. Sending Pictures, Emojis, and More (MMS)

Want to make your message more fun or personal?

Add a Picture

1. Tap the (Attach icon) or +.

2. Choose Gallery, take a photo, or pick a file.

3. Tap Send.

Add Emojis

- Click on the smiley face ☺ close the keyboard and select your favorite emoji.

Record or Send a Voice Message

- Tap and hold the microphone icon to record a voice note.

MMS uses mobile data if you're not on Wi-Fi—keep that in mind if you're watching your plan.

5. Using Chat Features (Like iMessage for Android)

If you're using Google Messages and your carrier supports it, you can enjoy:

- Typing indicators (see when someone's typing)
- Read receipts (see when it's read)
- Send over Wi-Fi or data

To Turn on Chat Features

1. Open Google Messages.
2. Simply tap on the three dots symbol (⋮) > Settings > Chat Functions.
3. Toggle Enable chat features ON.

Both you and the person you're messaging need to have chat features enabled to use them.

6. Reading and Replying to Messages

When you receive a message:

- You'll get a notification. Tap it to read.
- Open the Messages app to view conversations.
- Click on the chat to launch, then type and send your reply.

Missed messages? They're all saved in the Messages app—you can read them anytime.

7. Group Messaging

Text multiple people at once!

How to Start a Group Message

1. Open Messages and tap Start Chat.
2. Add multiple contacts.
3. Type your message and hit Send.

Everyone in the group can reply and see others' responses—just like a group chat.

8. Blocking Spam Texts

Tired of annoying messages?

Block a Number

1. Open the message.
2. And just tap on the three dots symbol (:) > Block number.

You can also report spam if needed.

Quick Recap Table

Task   How to Do It Notes

Sending SMS Messages > Start chat > Type > Send
Easy text messages

Send Picture (MMS) Tap > Gallery > Select > Send
Uses mobile data

Use Emojis   Tap 😊 on keyboard Add   fun
expressions

Chat Features (RCS) Google Messages > Settings >
Chat features Like iMessage, over Wi-Fi/data

Group Text   Add multiple contacts to a new
message   Great for family chats

Block Spam   Open message > ⋮ > Block number Stop
unwanted messages

Chapter Eight
Connecting to the Internet & Wi-Fi

Setting Up Mobile Data, Wi-Fi Networks, and Managing Connections

1. Two Ways to Get Online

Your Galaxy A16 connects to the internet in two main ways:

- Wi-Fi – Uses a home, public, or work wireless network. Usually free and doesn't use your data plan.
- Mobile Data – Uses your phone carrier's network. Works anywhere you have signal, but may affect your monthly data allowance.

Wi-Fi is usually the best choice at home to avoid using up mobile data.

2. Connecting to Wi-Fi

Let's get you online at home, a café, or anywhere with Wi-Fi.

How to Connect

1. To launch the Fast Settings panel Simply swipe down from the top of your screen.

2. Tap and hold the Wi-Fi icon.

3. Your smartphone will automatically scan for available networks.

4. Click on your network name (like "Home Wi-Fi").

5. Enter the password, then tap Connect.

You'll see a checkmark when it's connected!

Your phone remembers networks—no need to re-enter the password every time.

3. Turning Wi-Fi On or Off

Quick Method

- Swipe down two times to launch the Quick Settings, then click the Wi-Fi icon to activate or deactivate.

Turn off Wi-Fi when you're not using it to save battery if you're on mobile data.

4. Setting Up Mobile Data

Mobile data keeps you connected when you're outside Wi-Fi range.

Turn Mobile Data On

1. Launch the Settings > Connections > Data usage.

2. Toggle Mobile data to ON.

Quick Way

- Simply swipe down from the top and click on the Phone Mobile Data symbol.

You'll need a SIM card with an active data plan to use this feature.

5. Checking Data Usage

Worried about using too much?

See Your Usage

1. Navigate to the Settings > Connections > Data usage.

2. You'll see how much data you've used and what apps are using it.

Set a Data Limit

- Tap Billing cycle and data warning.

- Set a warning or limit to avoid going over your plan.

Pro tip: Set your phone to warn you before using too much data!

6. Switching Between Wi-Fi and Mobile Data Automatically

Your phone can switch to mobile data when Wi-Fi is weak:

1. Navigate to the Settings > Connections > Wi-Fi > Advanced.

2. Toggle Switch to mobile data ON.

This keeps you connected without you needing to do anything!

7. Using Airplane Mode

Airplane mode turns off all wireless connections.

To Turn It On/Off

- Swipe down from the top > click on the Airplane symbol.

Use this when flying or saving battery.

8. Sharing Your Connection: Mobile Hotspot

You can simply transfer or share your phone's mobile data with another device (like a tablet or laptop).

Turn on Mobile Hotspot

1. Pilot to the Settings > Connections > Phone Mobile Hotspot and Tethering.
2. Tap Mobile Hotspot > On.
3. Set up a name and password.

Now others can connect using your phone's internet!

Be careful—this uses your data quickly!

Quick Recap Table

Task   How to Do It Notes

Connect to Wi-Fi   Settings > Connections > Wi-FiFree, fast, doesn't use data plan

Turn on Mobile Data Settings > Data usage or Quick Settings   Needs SIM + active data plan

Check Data Usage   Settings > Data usage Helps avoid overage charges

Enable Hotspot   Settings > Mobile Hotspot Share internet with others

Airplane Mode   Click on the airplane symbol in Quick Settings   Turns off all wireless connections

You're now fully connected and in control of your phone's internet settings!

Chapter Nine
Mastering the Camera

Using Photo and Video Modes, Filters, Settings, and Tips for Great Shots

1. Opening the Camera App

Let's start with the basics!

- From the Home Screen, tap the Camera app.
- Or, swipe up from the bottom and find Camera in the app drawer.
- You can also double press the Side Key (power button) quickly to launch the camera anytime.

Tip: Practice launching it fast—you never know when a great moment pops up!

2. Exploring Camera Modes

Your Galaxy A16 offers several camera modes:

Mode   What It Does

Photo For everyday pictures

Video Records high-quality video

Portrait   Adds background blur for professional-looking shots

Pro   Manual settings for advanced users (optional)

More Might include Panorama, Macro, or Night Mode

Swipe left or right on the screen to switch between modes.

3. Taking Great Photos

In Photo Mode

1.   Aim your camera at the subject.

2.   Tap the screen to focus if needed.

3.   Click on the white shutter button to snap a photo.

That's it!

Want to take a selfie? Tap the camera flip icon 🔄 to switch to the front camera.

4. Using Filters and Effects

Add style to your shots instantly

- Tap the magic wand icon to access filters.

- Scroll through filters like Warm, Cool, Retro, etc.

- Tap one to preview, then snap your shot.

Play around—filters are great for mood and color!

5. Zoom In or Out

Pinch the screen outward to zoom in, inward to zoom out.

You can also use the zoom slider that appears on the screen.

Zoom reduces quality a little—get closer, if possible, for sharper results.

6. Video Recording Basics

1. Swipe to Video mode.

2. Tap the red record button to start filming.

3. Tap it again to stop.

Try to hold the phone steady or use a small tripod for smooth footage.

7. Adjusting Camera Settings

Tap the gear icon ⚙ (usually in the top corner of the Camera app) to open settings.

You can:

- Change photo resolution for more detail
- Turn on the grid lines to help frame shots
- Enable location tags
- Set a timer for hands-free shots

8. Tips for Better Photos

- Lighting stuffs – Normal light is really your best friend!
- Keep steady – Hold the phone with both hands.
- Use portrait mode for people or pets.
- Tap to focus before taking a photo.
- Clean your lens with a soft cloth before snapping pics!
- A clean lens = clearer photos!

9. Viewing & Editing Your Photos

View Photos

- Open the Gallery app or tap the thumbnail preview after taking a picture.

Edit a Photo

1. Open the photo in Gallery.
2. Tap the pencil icon or Edit.
3. Crop, adjust brightness, contrast, or apply filters.
4. Tap Save to keep the changes.

Don't worry—your original is usually saved too, just in case.

10. Deleting Unwanted Photos

- Launch the Gallery, touch and hold the picture.
- Tap Delete.
- Confirm to move it to the Trash (it stays there for 30 days before permanent removal).

Quick Recap Table

Task	How to Do It	Tips
Open Camera	Tap app, swipe up, or double press Side Key	Use shortcut for quick shots
Switch Modes	Swipe left/right in camera app	Try Portrait or Video
Use Filters	Tap in camera, pick a style	Preview before snapping
Record Video	Swipe to Video, tap red button	Hold steady or use a tripod
Edit Photos	Gallery > Edit (icon)	Crop, brighten, or filter
Delete Photos	Long press > Delete > Confirm	Photos stay in Trash for 30 days

You're now ready to capture memories like a pro—whether it's a family gathering, a beautiful sunset, or your pet doing something hilarious.

Chapter Ten
Using Apps and the Galaxy Store

Exploring Galaxy Store vs. Google Play

1. Install your Applications from Google Play Store

The Google Play Store is where you'll find millions of apps for entertainment, productivity, and more.

How to Install Apps

1. Open the Google Play Store app.

2. At the top click on the Search bar.

3. Type in the name of the application you like to download.

4. Tap the app you want, then tap Install.

Once installed, the app will appear on your home screen or in your app drawer!

Tip: Use the Play Store for almost all of your app needs—games, utilities, social media, and more.

2. Installing Apps from the Galaxy Store

The Galaxy Store is Samsung's app marketplace, offering exclusive apps, themes, and other Samsung-related content.

How to Install Apps

1. Open the Galaxy Store app.
2. Tap the Search bar or browse categories.
3. Find an app and tap it.
4. Tap Install.

Tip: The Galaxy Store is a great place for Samsung-specific apps like Samsung Health or Samsung Members, plus unique themes and icons.

3. Updating Your Apps

It's important to keep your apps up-to-date for the latest features and security improvements.

How to Update Apps (Google Play Store)

1. Open Google Play Store.
2. Tap the Menu icon (three lines).

3. Tap My apps & games.

4. Click on Update all to update every application, or update app individually by clicking Update next to the application.

Set automatic updates: In the Play Store, tap Settings > Auto-update apps, and choose Over Wi-Fi only or Any network.

How to Update Apps (Galaxy Store)

1. Open the Galaxy Store.

2. Tap the Menu icon (three lines).

3. Tap My apps.

4. Tap Update next to the apps you want to update or tap Update All.

Keeping apps updated helps avoid bugs and ensures better performance.

4. Organizing Apps on Your Home Screen

Organizing your apps makes it easier to find and use them. Let's clean up your home screen!

To Move Apps

1. Tap and hold the app icon.

2. Drag it to a new location on your home screen.

To Create Folders

1. Tap and hold an app icon.

2. Drag it over another app you want in the same folder.

3. The apps will combine into a folder.

4. Tap the folder to rename it (e.g., "Games," "Social").

5. Add more apps by dragging them into the folder.

Folders keep your home screen neat and organized!

5. Removing Unwanted Apps

If you want to delete an app you no longer use:

From the Home Screen

1. Tap and hold the app icon.

2. Tap Uninstall.

3. Confirm by tapping OK.

From the App Drawer

1. Open the App Drawer (swipe up on the home screen).
2. Tap and hold the app you want to uninstall.
3. Tap Uninstall and confirm.

Deleting an app removes it from your phone, but it doesn't delete your account or data (unless you specifically delete them from within the app).

6. Managing App Permissions

Some apps may ask for permissions (e.g., access to your camera, contacts, etc.). You can manage these at any time.

How to Manage Permissions

1. Navigate to the Settings > Apps.
2. Select the app you want to manage.
3. Tap Permissions.
4. Toggle permissions on/off based on what you want the app to access.

Review permissions regularly to ensure apps aren't accessing information you don't want to share.

7. Using App Notifications

Apps send notifications to alert you of new messages, reminders, or updates.

To Manage Notifications

1. Navigate to the Settings > Apps.
2. Tap on the app you want to adjust notifications for.
3. Tap Notifications and toggle them on/off.

Keep important notifications, but silence the ones you don't need.

8. Galaxy Store vs. Google Play Store

Both stores have different strengths—here's a quick comparison:

Feature	Google Play Store	Galaxy Store
App Variety	Access to millions of apps (games, tools, etc.)	Focuses on Samsung-specific apps and exclusive themes
Updates	Regular updates for a wide range of apps	Updates for Samsung apps and features

Payment Methods   Google Play balance, credit cards, etc.   Samsung account, carrier billing, etc.

Exclusives   Tons of third-party apps   Samsung-exclusive apps and features

Quick Recap Table

Task   How to Do It Tips

Installing Applications   Play Store or Galaxy Store > Search > Install   Play Store for general apps, Galaxy Store for Samsung-specific ones

Update Apps Google Play > Menu > My apps & games > Update all   Set auto-updates for convenience

Organize Apps   Hold app icon > Drag to rearrange or create folders Keep your home screen neat

Remove Apps Hold app icon > Uninstall   Free   up space by removing unused apps

Manage App Permissions   Settings > Apps > App > Permissions   Review app permissions regularly

Adjust Notifications Settings > Apps > App > Notifications Customize which alerts you receive

Chapter Eleven
Setting Up Email, Social Media Accounts, and Managing Notifications

Connecting Your Digital Life and Staying Notified

1. Setting Up Your Email Account

Stay connected by setting up your email account on your Galaxy A16.

To Set Up Gmail (Google Account)

1. Open the Email app.

2. Tap Add Account.

3. Select Google.

4. Enter your email address and password.

5. Tap Next, follow any on-screen instructions to complete the setup.

Once set up, you can send and receive emails directly from the Email app.

To Set Up Other Email Accounts

1. Open the Email app.

2. Tap Add Account.

3. Choose the email provider (e.g., Outlook, Yahoo).

4. Enter your email address and password.

5. Follow the instructions for your specific provider.

Your Galaxy A16 supports many popular email services like Yahoo, Outlook, and Exchange.

2. Setting Up Social Media Accounts

Social media applications enable you to connect with friends, family, and the world.

To Install and Set Up Facebook, Instagram, or Twitter

1. Start the Google Play Store or the Galaxy Store.

2. Search for the social media app (e.g., Facebook, Instagram, Twitter).

3. Tap Install.

4. Once installed, open the app.

5. Log in with your account credentials or create a new account if you don't have one.

Social media apps will notify you when you have messages, friend requests, or updates. Be ready to engage!

3. Managing Social Media Notifications

Stay in control of notifications from your social media apps. If it's a like on a post or a message from a friend, you can choose which notifications you like to see.

How to Manage Social Media Notifications

1. Open the Settings app.
2. Go to Apps > Manage Apps.
3. Find the social media app you want to adjust (e.g., Facebook, Instagram).
4. Click on the application, then choose Notifications.
5. Toggle the notifications on or off depending on your preference.

If you want only important notifications, like messages or comments, customize it for a cleaner experience.

4. Setting Up Email Notifications

You don't want to miss important emails. Here's how you can rightfully get the notifications:

For Gmail (Google Account)

1. Open the Gmail app.

2. In the top left corner, you can click on the three lines symbol ($\equiv$).

3. Scroll down and tap Settings.

4. Tap your email account.

5. Tap Notifications and select one of these options:

o All: Get notified about all emails.

o High priority only: Get notified about important emails.

For Other Email Accounts

1. Open the Email app.
2. Tap the three dots (:) in the top-right corner and select Settings.
3. Tap your email account.
4. Tap Notifications to adjust preferences.

Turn on Push Notifications to get instant updates for new emails.

5. Customizing App Notifications

You can fine-tune notifications for all apps, so you're only interrupted by the things that matter.

How to Customize Notifications for Any App

1. Open the Settings app.
2. Tap Notifications.
3. Scroll down and tap on an app (e.g., WhatsApp, Messenger).
4. Toggle off or on for specific types of notifications (e.g., message notifications, sound, vibration).

5. You can also customize the notification sound or set up Do Not Disturb when you need some quiet time.

Use Do Not Disturb to silence all calls and notifications when you need a break. Just go to Settings > Sounds and vibration > Do Not Disturb.

6. Adding More Accounts and Managing Multiple Accounts

Your Galaxy A16 allows you to add multiple accounts for email and social media apps.

To Add Another Email Account

1. Open the Email app.
2. Tap Add Account.
3. Select the email provider and sign in with another account.

To Add More Social Media Accounts

- Open the social media app (e.g., Instagram).
- Go to your profile, tap Settings, and look for the option to Add Account.

Easily switch between multiple accounts without needing to log out!

7. Managing Account Privacy and Security

Your social media accounts and email are valuable, so ensure they're safe and secure.

For Social Media Accounts

- Always enable Two-Factor Authentication (2FA) in the account settings for extra security.

- Regularly update your password and use a unique one for each account.

For Email Accounts

- Enable two-step verification for added protection.

- Use the Email app's encryption for sensitive emails (when supported).

Protect your accounts to avoid unauthorized access.

Quick Recap Table

Task	How to Do It	Tips
Set Up Email	Open Email app > Add Account	Use Gmail, Outlook, Yahoo, etc.
Set Up social media	Install app from Play Store > Log in	Stay connected with Facebook, Instagram, etc.
Manage Social Media Notifications	Settings > Apps > Social Media app > Notifications	Customize how often you're notified
Set Up Email Notifications	Gmail > Settings > Notifications	Get alerts for important emails
Customize App Notifications	Settings > Notifications > App	Silence unnecessary apps
Add More Accounts	Email app > Add Account / Social Media app	Switch between multiple accounts
Ensure Account Security	Enable Two-Factor Authentication (2FA)	Keep accounts safe and secure.

Chapter Twelve
Exploring Samsung Features

Maximizing Your Galaxy A16 Experience with Samsung's Exclusive Apps

1. Samsung Members: Your Support Hub

Samsung Members is your one-stop hub for getting support, tips, and tricks for your Galaxy A16.

Features of Samsung Members

- Diagnostics: Check your device's health with built-in diagnostics.

- Support: Get direct access to Samsung support for troubleshooting issues.

- Community: Join the Samsung community to discuss tips, news, and troubleshooting with other Galaxy users.

- Rewards: Earn points and get exclusive offers when you use Samsung services.

How to Use Samsung Members

1. Open the Samsung Members app (usually pre-installed).

2. To unlock all features just sign in with your Samsung account.

3. Browse through the app to explore Support, Community, and Rewards.

4. Tap on Diagnostics to run tests on your phone (e.g., battery health, camera, and screen check).

Samsung Members is great for support and keeping your Galaxy A16 running smoothly.

2. Smart Switch: Moving Your Data to Your New Phone

Switching to your new Galaxy A16 from an old phone? Smart Switch makes it easy to transfer everything—contacts, photos, messages, and apps—from your old device to your new one.

How to Use Smart Switch

1. Just download the Smart Switch on both smartphones (Galaxy or non-Galaxy).

2. Open Smart Switch on your new Galaxy A16.

3. Select the transfer method:

    o   Wireless: Use Wi-Fi to transfer data.

    o   Cable: Connect both phones with a USB cable and transfer your data quickly.

4. Select what you want to transfer (contacts, apps, music, etc.), then tap Send.

Smart Switch works with both Samsung and non-Samsung devices, making the switch smooth.

Tip:

*   If your old phone is an iPhone, you'll need to have your Apple ID and password to transfer data via Smart Switch.

3. Samsung Health: Track Your Wellness

Samsung Health is a powerful app to track your fitness, monitor your health, and stay motivated.

Key Features

- Activity Tracking: Tracks steps, exercise, and calories burned.

- Heart Rate Monitoring: Uses the Galaxy A16's sensors to measure heart rate.

- Sleep Tracking: Monitor your sleep patterns and get insights on how to improve your sleep.

- Stress Tracking: Helps you manage stress by measuring your stress levels.

How to Set Up Samsung Health

1. Open the Samsung Health app (pre-installed).

2. Sign in with your Samsung account (optional but recommended for syncing data).

3. Set up your profile by entering details like age, weight, height, and fitness goals.

4. Start tracking your activities by tapping Start Exercise and choosing from options like running, walking, or cycling.

5. Use the Heart Rate or Stress feature to get insights about your health.

Samsung Health is great for beginners looking to stay healthy without needing expensive fitness trackers.

4. Galaxy Themes: Personalize Your Phone

Galaxy Themes allows you to change the look and feel of your Galaxy A16, from wallpapers and icons to system sounds.

How to Change Your Theme

1. Open the Settings app.

2. Scroll down and tap Themes.

3. Browse the available themes or search for one by category (e.g., Nature, Abstract, or Minimalist).

4. Click on the theme you like to apply and then click Apply.

Customizing Other Aspects

- Wallpaper: Setting a custom wallpaper for your lock screen and home screen.

- Icons: Change your app icons for a different look.

- Ringtones and Sounds: Set unique ringtones and notification sounds for a personalized experience.

Galaxy Themes gives your phone a custom feel, and you can even create your own theme if you prefer!

Chapter Thirteen
Security and Privacy Settings

Securing Your Galaxy A16 and Keeping Your Personal Data Safe

1. Setting Up Fingerprint Security

Fingerprint recognition is one of the most convenient ways to unlock your Galaxy A16. It's fast, secure, and easy to set up.

How to Set Up Fingerprint Unlock

1. Pilot to the Settings > Biometrics and security > Fingerprints.

2. Tap Add fingerprint.

3. Follow the on-screen instructions to place your finger on the fingerprint sensor located on the back of the phone (or wherever specified on your model).

4. Please ensure to lift and place your finger in different positions on the sensor until it's fully registered.

Tip: Make sure your fingers are clean and dry when setting up your fingerprint for best results.

Using Fingerprint to Unlock

- Once set up, simply touch the fingerprint sensor to unlock your phone or authorize secure actions (like payments or app access).

2. Setting Up Face Unlock

Face recognition is another fast and secure way to unlock your phone, especially useful when you don't want to touch the phone.

How to Set Up Face Unlock

1. Pilot to the Settings > Biometrics and security > Face recognition.
2. Tap Register face.
3. Hold your phone at eye level and follow the on-screen instructions to capture your face. Please ensure you're in a well-lit area.
4. After registering, your phone will automatically use your face to unlock when you look at it.

Tip: For added security, set a backup unlock method (like a PIN or pattern) in case your face isn't recognized.

3. Setting Up a Password, PIN, or Pattern

For those who prefer traditional security methods, you can set up a PIN, password, or pattern lock.

Set Up a PIN, Password, or Pattern

1. Pilot to the Settings > Biometrics and security > Screen lock type.

2. Choose from the following options:

   o PIN: Enter a 4–6-digit PIN that you'll need to enter every time you unlock your phone.

   o Password: Choose a more complex password (letters and numbers) for stronger security.

   o Pattern: Draw a pattern using your finger on the screen.

3. Follow the on-screen prompts to set up your chosen lock method.

Tip: Make sure your PIN or password isn't something easy to guess (e.g., 1234 or your birthday).

How to Set Up Find My Mobile

1. Pilot to the Settings > Biometrics and security > Find My Mobile.

2. Sign in with your Samsung account.

3. Make sure Remote unlock and send last location is enabled so your phone can be tracked and unlocked remotely if needed.

Tip: In case of theft or loss, go to the Find My Mobile website to locate and remotely control your device.

6. Two-Factor Authentication (2FA)

To add extra protection to your accounts, you should enable two-factor authentication (2FA) for apps like your email, banking, or social media accounts.

How to Enable 2FA

1. Launch the application where you like to activate 2FA (e.g., Google, Facebook, Samsung account).

2. Navigate to the account settings and find Security or Two-step verification.

3. Follow the on-screen steps to link your phone number or use an authentication app (like Google Authenticator).

4. After enabling 2FA, you'll need to enter a verification code sent to your phone or generated by an app in addition to your regular password.

2FA provides an extra layer of security for your online accounts.

7. Encrypting Your Phone for Extra Security

If you want to add an extra layer of protection, you can encrypt your Galaxy A16. This makes the data on your phone unreadable to anyone who doesn't have the proper key (PIN, password, or biometric).

How to Enable Encryption

1. Navigate to the Settings > Biometrics and security > Encryption.

2. Follow the prompts to set up encryption if it's not already enabled.

Note: Encryption is automatically enabled on most devices, but if you want to double-check, you can do it manually here.

8. Protecting Your Data with App Permissions

Some applications request access to your camera, microphone, location, or other sensitive data. You can simply as well manage application permissions to control what each app can access.

How to Manage App Permissions

1. Pilot to the Settings > Apps > Select the app you want to manage.
2. Tap Permissions.
3. Toggle the permissions you like to enable or deny (e.g., Camera, Microphone, Location).

Tip: Regularly review app permissions to make sure apps aren't accessing more data than they need.

9. Using a VPN for Added Privacy

A VPN (Virtual Private Network) helps protect your online activity by encrypting your internet connection.

How to Set Up a VPN

1. Download a trusted VPN app from the Google Play Store (e.g., ExpressVPN, NordVPN).

2. Follow the on-screen setup instructions and log in.

3. Activate the VPN whenever you like to secure your internet connection.

Tip: A VPN is essential for privacy when using public Wi-Fi in cafes or airports.

Quick Recap Table

Task	How to Do It	Tips
Set Up Fingerprint Unlock	Settings > Biometrics and security > Fingerprints	Clean and dry finger for best results

Set Up Face Unlock Settings > Biometrics and security > Face recognition Add a backup PIN for security

Set Up PIN, Password, or Pattern Settings > Biometrics and security > Screen lock type Use a strong, unique password/PIN

Use Secure Folder Settings > Biometrics and security > Secure Folder Protect sensitive files and apps

Enable Find My Mobile Settings > Biometrics and security > Find My Mobile Track your phone if lost or stolen

Enable Two-Factor Authentication Account settings > Security > Two-step verification Add extra security to your accounts

Encrypt Your Phone Settings > Biometrics and security > Encryption Encrypt to protect data from unauthorized access

Manage Application Permissions   Settings > Apps > App > Permissions   Control what applications can access your information

Set Up a VPN Download VPN app from Google Play, follow setup   Use VPN for secure browsing on public Wi-Fi

Your Galaxy A16 is now fully protected with biometric security, passwords, and encryption!

Chapter Fourteen
Managing Storage and Files

Keeping Your Galaxy A16 Organized and Running Smoothly

1. Using the File Manager

The File Manager is a built-in app on your Galaxy A16 that helps you organize and manage your files like photos, videos, documents, and downloads.

How to Use the File Manager

1. Open the My Files app from the Apps screen.
2. You'll see categories like Images, Audio, Documents, Downloads, and SD Card.
3. Tap on any category to view the files.
4. You can move, copy, delete, or rename files directly within the app.

Tip: Use the Search feature at the top to quickly find specific files.

How to Organize Your Files

- Create Folders: Tap the three dots (⋮) in the top right corner and select Create Folder.

- Move Files: Select the files you want to move, tap the three dots (⋮), and choose Move. Select the destination folder.

Organizing your files makes it easier to find what you need and helps your phone run more smoothly.

2. Managing the SD Card

Your Galaxy A16 supports SD cards for extra storage, allowing you to keep photos, videos, and documents without taking up space on your phone's internal storage.

Inserting and Removing an SD Card

1. Locate the SIM/SD card tray on the side of your Galaxy A16.
2. Use the SIM ejector tool (or a small pin) to eject the tray.
3. Place your SD card in the designated slot and insert the tray back into your phone.

Tip: Ensure the SD card is properly aligned before inserting it to avoid damage.

How to Manage Files on the SD Card

1. Open the My Files app and tap SD Card to view its contents.

2. You can move or copy files between the SD card and your phone's internal storage to free up space.

3. If you no longer need a file on the SD card, simply delete it from the SD card folder.

Tip: Move large files like videos and photos to your SD card to save internal storage space.

3. Cloud Backups: Keep Your Data Safe

Cloud backups ensure that your important data, like photos, contacts, and app data, are safe even if you lose or damage your phone.

How to Back Up Using Google Drive

1. Launch the Google Drive app (pre-installed on most Galaxy devices).

2. Sign in with your Google account if you haven't already.

3. Click on the plus sign (+) and select Upload to back up files (e.g., photos, videos, or documents).

4. You can also set up automatic backups for photos and videos using Google Photos.

How to Back Up Using Samsung Cloud

1. Navigate to the Settings > Accounts and backup > Samsung Cloud.

2. Tap Back up data.

3. Select what you want to back up (contacts, calendar, photos, etc.), then tap Back up now.

Tip: Samsung Cloud offers a more integrated backup for Galaxy devices, but Google Drive is also a great option for universal cloud storage.

How to Restore from Google Drive or Samsung Cloud

- If you need to restore data after resetting or replacing your phone, sign in to your Google or Samsung account and choose Restore from backup during the setup process.

4. Freeing Up Space on Your Galaxy A16

Over time, your phone's storage can get filled with apps, photos, and files. Here's how to free up space and keep your phone running smoothly.

How to Check Storage Usage

1. Navigate to the Settings > Battery and device care > Storage.

2. You'll see a breakdown of how your storage is being used, including categories like Apps, Photos, Videos, and Audio.

How to Free Up Space

1. Clear App Cache: Tap on Apps in the Storage menu, select an app, and tap Storage. From here, you can tap Clear Cache to free up space without deleting the app.

2. Uninstall Unused Apps: Tap Apps, find apps you no longer use, and tap Uninstall.

3. Delete Old Photos or Videos: Open the Gallery app, go through old photos or videos, and delete the ones you no longer need. You can

also move them to your SD card or Google Photos for safe storage.

Tip: Use Google Photos to store unlimited photos and videos online for free (high quality), which helps you free up space on your device.

How to Use the Device Care Tool

1. Navigate to the Settings > Battery and device care > Storage.

2. Tap Clean Now to automatically remove temporary files, cache, and other unnecessary data.

Tip: Run the Device Care tool regularly to keep your phone clean and organized.

5. Using Third-Party Apps for Cleaning and Organizing

If you prefer a more thorough clean-up, you can download third-party apps like CCleaner or Files by Google from the Google Play Store to help with storage management.

How to Use Files by Google

1. Under the Play Store download Files by Google.

2. Open the app and tap on Clean to identify unused files, duplicate files, and cache data.

3. Tap Free up space to remove unnecessary files.

Tip: Be cautious when using third-party apps—make sure they are trusted and have good reviews.

Quick Recap Table

Task	How to Do It	Tips
Use File Manager files by category	Open My Files app and organize file finding	Use the Search feature for quick
Manage SD Card to manage it save internal space	Insert SD card, use My Files app Move photos and videos to SD card to	
Cloud Backups Cloud to back up data unlimited photo storage	Use Google Drive or Samsung Use Google Photos for	

Free Up Space   Navigate to the Settings >
Storage, uninstall apps or clear cache   Use Google
Photos for cloud-based photo storage

Clean and Organize with Apps   Use   third-party
apps like Files by Google   Run the Device Care tool
regularly

By managing your files, using cloud backups, and
freeing up space, you'll keep your Galaxy A16 running
smoothly and your data safe!

Chapter Fifteen
Using Google Services

Harnessing the Power of Google's Services on Your Galaxy A16

1. Getting Started with Google Assistant

Google Assistant is your personal voice assistant that helps you perform tasks hands-free. Whether you need to set reminders, send messages, get directions, or control smart home devices, Google Assistant is here to help.

How to Set Up Google Assistant

1. Open the Google Assistant app or press and hold the Home button.

2. Follow the on-screen instructions to set up voice recognition and customize settings.

3. You can also say "Hey Google" or "OK Google" to activate Assistant whenever your phone is awake.

Common Google Assistant Commands

- Setting the Reminders: "Hey Google, please kindly remind me to call Mom later at 5 PM."

- Sending Messages: "Hey Google, please kindly send a message to John by saying I'll be there in 10 minutes time."

- Getting Instructions: "Hey Google, how long will it take to get to the closest coffee shop?"

- Controlling Smart Devices: "Hey Google, please put off the lights in the living room."

Tip: Customize your Google Assistant by going to Settings > Google > Assistant to choose your preferences, like voice, language, and more.

2. Using Gmail for Email Communication

Gmail is Google's email service, and it's pre-installed on your Galaxy A16. It's easy to set up and offers a powerful, organized way to manage your emails.

How to Set Up Gmail

1. Open the Gmail app.
2. Sign in with your Google account (or create a new account if you don't have one).
3. Once signed in, your inbox will automatically sync with your email account.

How to Use Gmail

- Compose Emails: Tap the plus sign (+) to start a new email, add a recipient, subject, and message.
- Organize Emails: Use Labels (like Inbox, Sent, Drafts) to categorize your messages and keep everything organized.
- Search: Tap the search bar at the top to quickly find specific emails.

Tip: Turn on Notifications for Gmail to get alerted when new emails arrive.

3. Navigating with Google Maps

Google Maps is your go-to navigation app for getting directions, exploring new places, and avoiding traffic.

How to Set Up Google Maps

1. Open the Google Maps app.

2. Sign in with your Google account to save your locations, routes, and favorite places.

3. Enable Location Services in your phone's settings to allow Google Maps to access your location for accurate directions.

Using Google Maps for Directions

- Get Directions: Tap the search bar, type the address or place name, then tap Directions. Choose your preferred mode of transportation (car, walking, public transport).

- Explore Nearby: Tap the Explore tab to find nearby restaurants, cafes, gas stations, and more.

- Save Locations: Tap Save on any location you visit often, such as home or work, to get easy access later.

Tip: You can download offline maps for areas with limited internet connection by tapping Offline Maps in the app's menu.

4. Storing and Sharing Files with Google Drive

Google Drive is your cloud storage service for storing files, photos, and documents that you can access from any device.

How to Set Up Google Drive

1. Open the Google Drive app.
2. Sign in with your Google account (or create one if you don't have one yet).
3. Once signed in, you'll have access to 15 GB of free storage space.

How to Use Google Drive

- Upload Files: Tap the plus sign (+) and choose Upload to add files from your phone.
- Create Documents: Tap + and select Google Docs, Google Sheets, or Google Slides to create new documents, spreadsheets, or presentations directly in Drive.
- Share Files: Select the file you want to share, tap the three dots (:), and choose Share to send it via email or get a shareable link.

Tip: You can organize your files in folders to keep everything neat in Google Drive.

5. Syncing Your Google Account for Seamless Experience

Syncing your Google account ensures that your emails, contacts, calendar events, and settings are backed up and stay consistent across all your devices.

How to Sync Your Google Account

1. Navigate to the Settings > Accounts and backup > Accounts > Google.

2. Check your battery usage: Navigate to the Settings > Battery & device care > Battery to see which apps are using the most power.

3. Adjust screen brightness: Set your screen brightness to automatically or manually decrease. Navigate to the Settings > Display > Brightness.

4. Turn off unnecessary features: Turn off features like Bluetooth, Wi-Fi, and location services when you're not using them. You can disable these features in Quick Settings.

5. Enable battery saver: To extend your battery life, enable battery saver in Settings > Battery & device care > Battery > Battery saver.

6. Disable background apps: Navigate to the Settings > Battery & device care > Background apps and disable apps you don't need running in the background.

7. Limit push mail sending: If you send mail via push (constantly checking for new mail), switch the feature to Manual or Retrieve. Go to Settings > Accounts & backup > Accounts > Select your email account > Sync settings.

TIP: If you notice a significant decrease in battery life, check which apps were recently updated. Sometimes new app versions can significantly drain your battery.

4. Fix connectivity issues (WiFi, mobile data, Bluetooth)

Connectivity issues can make it difficult to use your phone to make calls, surf the web, or perform other tasks. How to fix common issues:

Steps to fix WiFi connection issues

1. Turn Wi-Fi on and off: Swipe down from the top of the screen to open Quick Settings. Tap Wi-Fi to turn it off, wait a few seconds, then turn it back on.

2. Forget Wi-Fi and reconnect: Navigate to the Settings > Connections > Wi-Fi, tap the network name, and select Forget. Next, reconnect to the network by selecting the network again and entering the password.

3. Check your router settings: Restart your router to make sure it's working properly. You can also check your router settings (via its IP address) to make sure there's nothing wrong with the router.

4. Change WiFi band: Some routers offer 2.4GHz and 5GHz bands. If you're having connection issues, try using a different band. Navigate to the Settings > Connections > Wi-Fi > Advanced and switch bands.

Steps to fix your mobile data connection

1. Check your mobile data: Navigate to the Settings > Connections > Mobile networks and make sure mobile data is enabled.

2. Restart your phone: Sometimes a simple restart can help restore your mobile data connection.

3. Check your APN settings: If you're still having issues, check your APN (Access Point Name) settings. These dictate how your phone connects to the mobile network. Contact your mobile provider to get the correct APN settings.

4. Enable airplane mode: Turn airplane mode on for 30 seconds, then off again to refresh the connection.

Steps to fix Bluetooth connection issues

1. Turn Bluetooth off and back on: Open Quick Settings, tap Bluetooth to turn the feature off, wait a few seconds, then turn it back on.

2. Forget and reconnect the device: Go to Settings > Connections > Bluetooth, tap the device name, and select Forget. Then reconnect to the device.

3. Restart your phone and device: If you're still having issues, restart your phone and the Bluetooth device you're trying to connect to.

Tip: Make sure your Bluetooth device is in pairing mode and in range when trying to connect.

5. You can reset your network settings (if the issue continues)

If you're still having connection issues, you can reset your network settings. This will delete saved Wi-Fi networks, paired Bluetooth devices, and other network configurations.

To reset network settings

1. Navigate to the Settings > General management > Reset > Reset network settings.

2. Confirm the action. Your phone will now reset all network-related settings.

Tip: Resetting network settings can solve many connection problems, but it will delete saved Wi-Fi passwords and Bluetooth connections.

Quick Overview

Problem Solving

Tip

Phone Frozen/Unresponsive: Restart your phone, close unused apps, clear app cache. Restart your phone regularly to keep it up to date.

Poor performance: Close apps, clear cache, uninstall unused apps, use device maintenance. Disable animations for faster response time.

Battery usage: Check battery usage, adjust brightness, disable background apps. Activate power saving mode if necessary.

WiFi connection issues: Switch WiFi, forget connection and reconnect, check router settings. You can simply change between the 2.4 GHz and 5 GHz bands.

Mobile Data Connectivity Issues Check mobile data settings, restart phone, check APN settings Toggle Airplane Mode to refresh connection

Bluetooth Issues Toggle Bluetooth, forget and reconnect devices, restart phone and Bluetooth device Ensure device is in pairing mode and within range

By following these steps, you can troubleshoot and fix many common issues related to freezing, performance, battery drain, and connectivity on your Galaxy A16.

Chapter Sixteen
Troubleshooting Common Issues

Troubleshooting Common Issues on Your Galaxy A16

1. Fixing Freezing or Unresponsive Phone

If your Galaxy A16 freezes or becomes unresponsive, don't panic. It can often be fixed quickly with a few simple steps.

Steps to Fix Freezing

1. Restart Your Phone: The first step is to restart your phone to refresh the system. Press and hold the Power button carefully until the power options display and then choose Restart.

2. Close Unused Apps: Too many apps running in the background can slow your phone down and cause freezing. Swipe up from the bottom of the screen to view your recent apps and swipe away any you're not using.

3. Clear App Cache: Some apps may have too much stored data, causing your phone to freeze. Navigate to the Settings > Apps > Choose the application causing issues > Storage > Clear Cache.

4. Update Software: Freezing can also be due to outdated software. Navigate to the Settings > Software update > Download and install to check for any updates.

Tip: If your phone continues to freeze, you might want to do a factory reset (be sure to back up your data first).

2. Fixing Slow Performance

A slow phone can be frustrating, but there are several easy ways to improve performance.

Steps to Speed Up Your Phone

1. Close Unused Apps: Just like freezing, having many apps running in the background can slow down your phone. Close apps you're not actively using.

2. Clear Cache: Cached data can accumulate and slow down your device. Navigate to the Settings > Storage > Cached data > Clear cached data.

3. Uninstall Unnecessary Apps: If you have apps that you no longer use, uninstall them to free up space and resources. Navigate to the Settings > Applications, choose the app, and click on Uninstall.

4. Disable Animations: To make your phone feel snappier, disable animations. Navigate to the Settings > About phone > Tap Build number 7 times to enable Developer options. Then, move to Settings > Developer options > Window transition scale and Animator duration scale. Set both to Off.

5. Use Device Care: Navigate to the Settings > Battery and device care > Optimize now to help clean up files and optimize your phone's performance.

6. Free Up Space: If your phone is full, it can slow down. Navigate to the Settings > Battery and

device care > Storage to see what's taking up space and clear out unnecessary files.

Tip: Consider using Files by Google or CCleaner for more thorough cleaning and optimizing.

3. Solving Battery Drain Problems

Battery drain can occur if you have too many power-hungry apps running or if your phone's settings aren't optimized. Here's how to fix it:

Steps to Fix Battery Drain

1. Check Battery Usage: Navigate to the Settings > Battery and device care > Battery to see which apps are consuming the most battery.

2. Adjust Screen Brightness: Set your screen brightness to auto or lower it manually. Navigate to the Settings > Display > Brightness.

3. Turn Off Unnecessary Features: Disable features like Bluetooth, Wi-Fi, and Location Services when you're not using them. You can toggle these off in the Quick Settings menu.

4. Enable Power Saving Mode: To extend battery life, enable Power saving mode by going to Settings > Battery and device care > Battery > Power saving mode.

5. Turn Off Background Apps: Navigate to the Settings > Battery and device care > Background apps and toggle off apps that you don't need running in the background.

6. Limit Push Email: If you have email set to push (constantly checking for new emails), switch it to manual or fetch. Navigate to the Settings > Accounts and backup > Accounts > Select your email account > Sync settings.

Tip: If you notice a significant drop in battery life, check for apps that have been updated recently. Sometimes, a new version of an app can cause battery drain.

4. Resolving Connectivity Problems (Wi-Fi, Mobile Data, Bluetooth)

Connectivity issues can make it hard to use your phone for calls, browsing, and other tasks. Here's how to fix common issues:

Steps to Fix Wi-Fi Connectivity

1. Toggle Wi-Fi Off and On: Swipe down from the top of the screen to open Quick Settings. Tap Wi-Fi to turn it off, wait a few seconds, and then turn it back on.

2. Forget and reconnect to Wi-Fi: Navigate to the Settings > Connections > Wi-Fi, tap the network name, then select Forget. Afterward, reconnect to the network by selecting it again and entering the password.

3. Check Router Settings: Ensure your router is working correctly by restarting it. You can also check the router's settings (via its IP address) to ensure no issues on the router's end.

4. Change Wi-Fi Frequency Band: Some routers offer 2.4 GHz and 5 GHz bands. If you're

having trouble connecting, try switching to a different band. Navigate to the Settings > Connections > Wi-Fi > Advanced and toggle between bands.

Steps to Fix Mobile Data Connectivity

1. Check Mobile Data: Navigate to the Settings > Connections > Mobile networks to make sure Mobile data is turned on.

2. Restart Your Phone: Sometimes, a simple restart can help re-establish mobile data connectivity.

3. Check APN Settings: If you're still having trouble, check your APN settings (Access Point Name), which tell your phone how to connect to your mobile network. For the correct APN settings call your carrier.

4. Toggle Airplane Mode: Turn Airplane mode on for 30 seconds, then turn it off to refresh your connection.

Steps to Fix Bluetooth Connectivity

1. Toggle Bluetooth Off and On: Open Quick Settings, tap Bluetooth to turn it off, wait a few seconds, and then turn it back on.

2. Forget and Reconnect Devices: Navigate to the Settings > Connections > Bluetooth, tap the device name, then select Forget. Afterward, reconnect to the device.

3. Restart Your Phone and Device: If you're still having issues, restart both your phone and the Bluetooth device you're trying to connect to.

Tip: Ensure your Bluetooth device is in pairing mode and within range when trying to connect.

5. Resetting Network Settings (If Problems Persist)

If you continue to experience connectivity issues, you can reset your network settings, which will clear saved Wi-Fi networks, paired Bluetooth devices, and other network configurations.

How to Reset Network Settings

1. Navigate to the Settings > General management > Reset > Reset network settings.
2. Confirm the action, and your phone will reset all network-related settings.

Tip: Resetting network settings can resolve many connectivity issues but will erase saved Wi-Fi passwords and Bluetooth connections.

Quick Recap Table

Problem	How to Fix It	Tips
Freezing/Unresponsive Phone	Restart phone, close unused apps, clear app cache	Regularly restart your phone to keep it fresh
Slow Performance	Close apps, clear cache, uninstall unused apps, use Device Care	Disable animations for faster response times
Battery Drain	Check battery usage, adjust brightness, turn off background apps	Enable Power Saving Mode when necessary

Wi-Fi Connectivity Issues   Toggle Wi-Fi, forget and reconnect to network, check router settings   Try switching between 2.4 GHz and 5 GHz bands

Mobile Data Connectivity Issues   Check   mobile data settings, restart phone, check APN settings Toggle Airplane Mode to refresh connection

Bluetooth Issues   Toggle Bluetooth, forget and reconnect devices, restart phone and Bluetooth device Ensure device is in pairing mode and within range

By following these steps, you can troubleshoot and fix many common issues related to freezing, performance, battery drain, and connectivity on your Galaxy A16.

Chapter Seventeen
Maintenance and Software Updates

Maintaining a Healthy and Efficient Galaxy A16

1. Keeping Your Phone Updated

Regular updates ensure that your phone's software is up-to-date with the latest features, security patches, and bug fixes. Here's how to keep your Galaxy A16 running smoothly with updates:

How to Check for Software Updates

1. Navigate to the Settings > Software update.

2. Tap Download and install to check for any available updates.

3. If an update is available, tap Download and follow the on-screen instructions to install it.

Tip: It's a good idea to connect your phone to Wi-Fi and ensure it has enough battery (or plug it into a charger) before installing updates.

What Updates Include

- Security Patches: These updates fix security vulnerabilities to keep your device safe.

- Bug Fixes: Updates often fix bugs or glitches that may affect your phone's performance.

- New Features: Some updates introduce new features and improvements to the system and apps.

- Performance Enhancements: Updates can make your phone run smoother and faster.

Setting Up Automatic Updates

1. Navigate to the Settings > Software update.

2. Enable Auto-download over Wi-Fi to automatically download updates when connected to Wi-Fi.

3. Turn on Install updates automatically so updates install when they're ready, without you having to manually do it.

Tip: If you're having issues after an update, check the software update section for Update History to see what was changed.

2. Factory Resetting Your Phone

If your phone is experiencing ongoing issues or you want to start fresh, a factory reset can be a solution. A factory reset erases all data from your device and restores it to its original state when it was first purchased.

When to Perform a Factory Reset

- Your phone is running very slowly despite troubleshooting.
- You're selling or giving away your phone and want to remove all personal data.
- Your phone is constantly freezing or having major issues that can't be solved by other means.

How to Perform a Factory Reset

1. Backup Your Data: Before resetting, it's important to back up your data (photos, contacts, apps, etc.) to Google Drive, Samsung Cloud, or an external storage device.
2. Navigate to the Settings > General management > Reset.

3. Tap Factory data reset and read the information carefully. This will erase everything on your phone, including apps, settings, and personal data.

4. Tap Reset and confirm your choice. You may be asked to enter your PIN, password, or pattern to proceed.

5. Once the reset is complete, your phone will restart, and you'll be guided through the initial setup process.

Warning: A factory reset is permanent. Make sure you back up all important data before proceeding.

3. Using Device Care Features

Your Galaxy A16 comes with a set of Device Care features that can help you maintain your phone's performance and keep it running smoothly.

How to Access Device Care

1. Navigate to the Settings > Battery and device care.

2. Here, you can find a variety of tools to optimize your phone's performance.

Key Features of Device Care

1. Optimize Now:

o This feature checks your device for any performance issues, such as apps using too much memory, battery, or storage.

o Tap Optimize now to let the system automatically perform a clean-up and optimize your phone's performance.

Tip: Use this feature regularly to ensure your phone runs efficiently.

2. Battery

o Tap on Battery to see your phone's current battery usage and get tips on how to save power.

o You can also enable Power saving mode to extend battery life, reduce background activity, and limit certain features.

Tip: Use Battery usage to check which apps are consuming the most battery and consider uninstalling or limiting background activity for power-hungry apps.

3. Storage

o Check the remaining storage space on your smartphone.

o Tap Clean now to clear unnecessary files and free up space.

o You can also tap Manage storage to see which apps or files are taking up the most space and delete or move them as needed.

Tip: Regularly check storage to avoid running out of space, which can slow down your phone.

4. Memory

o This section shows how much RAM (memory) is being used and which apps are using the most memory.

o You can tap Clean now to close unused apps and free up memory, improving your phone's performance.

Tip: If apps are frequently slowing down your phone, consider uninstalling or limiting background activity in settings.

5. Security

o Device Care will also check for any security vulnerabilities. It scans for malicious apps, outdated software, or privacy risks.

o Tap Scan phone to run a quick security check, and ensure your phone is protected.

Tip: Always keep your phone's security settings updated, including using Fingerprint or Face unlock for enhanced security.

6. Device Protection

o Enable Find My Mobile through Samsung's service, so you can track your phone if it gets lost or stolen.

o You can also enable Remote lock or Wipe data in case your device is compromised.

4. Managing Updates, Backups, and Data

To ensure everything is up to date, secure, and backed up, here are a few more tips:

Backup Your Data Regularly

- Use Samsung Cloud, Google Drive, or other cloud services to back up your important data like photos, contacts, and apps.

- Navigate to the Settings > Accounts and backup > Backup and restore to configure your backup settings.

Manage Updates

- As mentioned in Keeping Your Phone Updated, keeping your software and apps updated is essential for performance and security.

- Update Apps: Go to Google Play Store or Galaxy Store and make sure all your apps are up to date.

Check for App-Specific Updates

- If you notice an app acting up or crashing frequently, check for updates in the Play Store or Galaxy Store.

Quick Recap Table

Task	How to Do It	Tips
Check for Software Updates	Navigate to the Settings > Software update > Download and install	Enable Auto-download over Wi-Fi for convenience
Factory Reset	Navigate to the Settings > General management > Reset > Factory data reset	Back up data before resetting to avoid loss
Optimize Phone	Navigate to the Settings > Battery and device care > Optimize now	Use Device Care regularly for smooth performance

Battery Management   Navigate to the Settings > Battery and device care > Battery   Enable   Power saving mode to extend battery life

Storage Management   Navigate to the Settings > Battery and device care > Storage   Use Clean now to free up storage space

Security Check   Navigate to the Settings > Battery and device care > Security   Run a phone scan regularly for security issues

By using the Device Care features, keeping your phone updated, and performing a factory reset when needed, you can ensure that your Galaxy A16 stays efficient, secure, and optimized for daily use.

Chapter Eighteen
Helpful Tips and Tricks

Unlock the Full Potential of Your Galaxy A16 with These Advanced Tips

1. Hidden Features of the Galaxy A16

Your Galaxy A16 comes with several hidden features that can make your experience smoother and more efficient. Let's uncover some of them!

One-Handed Mode

If your phone feels too big to use with one hand, enable One-Handed Mode to make the screen smaller and more manageable.

- Navigate to the Settings > Advanced features > One-handed mode and toggle it on.

- To activate it, swipe down diagonally from the bottom corners of the screen, and the display will shrink to a more accessible size.

App Pair

App Pair allows you to open two apps simultaneously in a split-screen view for multitasking.

- Launch the Recent Apps, select two apps that you want to use together, and tap the App Pair icon to create a shortcut for future use.

Edge Panels

Edge Panels are a quick way to access your favorite apps, tools, or features from the side of your screen.

- Navigate to the Settings > Display > Edge screen > Edge panels, and toggle it on. You can customize which panels you want to appear, such as apps, contacts, or clipboard.

Floating Apps

Make any app a floating window that you can drag around the screen, perfect for multitasking.

- Launch the Recent Apps, and tap the floating icon on any app you want to make float.

Tip: Enable Developer options by tapping Build number 7 times in About phone to unlock even more advanced features!

2. Useful Shortcuts for Speedy Navigation

Master these shortcuts to navigate your Galaxy A16 more efficiently!

Quick App Switching

Switch between the two most recently used apps quickly.

- Double-tap the Recent Apps button to toggle between apps.

Take a Screenshot

Capture your screen with ease.

- Press Power button + Volume Down button at the same time.
- For a scrolling screenshot, after taking a screenshot, tap Capture more to capture the entire screen or web page.

Quick Settings Panel

Open the Quick Settings by swiping down from the top of the screen, and swipe down again to access more settings like Battery, Wi-Fi, and Bluetooth. To toggle a setting quickly, simply tap on it.

Split Screen Mode

Use Split Screen to view two apps at once.

- Launch the Recent Apps, tap the app icon at the top, and select Open in split screen view.

Quick Access to Camera

Launch your camera instantly, even from the lock screen.

- Double-tap the Power button to open the Camera app, no need to unlock the phone first!

3. Battery-Saving Hacks to Maximize Battery Life

Extend the life of your battery with these clever tricks!

Turn on Power Saving Mode

Power Saving Mode reduces background activity, screen brightness, and animations to extend battery life.

- Navigate to the Settings > Battery and device care > Battery > Power saving mode to enable it.

- Use Medium Power Saving or Maximum Power Saving depending on your needs.

Limit Background Apps

Close unused apps and limit background processes to save battery.

- Navigate to the Settings > Battery and device care > Battery > Background apps to manage what runs in the background.

Disable Auto-Sync

Auto-sync drains battery by constantly syncing apps like email, contacts, and calendars. Turn it off for apps you don't need to sync constantly.

- Navigate to the Settings > Accounts and backup > Accounts, select the account, and toggle off Auto-sync for apps you don't need updating in real-time.

Use Dark Mode

Dark Mode not only saves battery on AMOLED displays but also makes the screen easier on the eyes.

- Navigate to the Settings > Display > Dark mode to enable it. Your phone will automatically use less power, especially with darker backgrounds in apps.

Turn Off Vibration

Vibration uses more battery than just ringing. Turn off vibration for notifications and calls to save power.

- Navigate to the Settings > Sound and vibration, and turn off Vibrate on touch and vibrate for calls.

Limit Location Services

Constantly using GPS can drain your battery. To essential applications only you can limit location services.

- Navigate to the Settings > Location, and turn off Use location or set it to Battery saving mode.

Customize Your Notifications

Get your notifications exactly the way you want by customizing them for each app.

- Navigate to the Settings > Notifications, and tap on an app to change notification settings, including sounds, vibrations, and whether notifications appear on the lock screen.

Set Up Secure Folders

Secure Folder lets you store private files and apps in a password-protected space on your phone.

- Navigate to the Settings > Biometrics and security > Secure Folder and follow the setup instructions.

Use the Digital Wellbeing Features

Track your screen time and set app limits to promote healthy phone usage.

- Navigate to the Settings > Digital Wellbeing & Parental Controls to see your screen time, set app timers, or enable Focus mode to reduce distractions.

Enable Developer Options for Extra Features

Unlock hidden features and advanced settings by enabling Developer options.

- Navigate to the Settings > About phone > Tap Build number 7 times to unlock Developer options.
- In Developer options, you can tweak animation scales, set up USB debugging, and even simulate a color blindness mode.

Create Custom Routines with Bixby Routines

Bixby Routines automates certain tasks based on your habits and context.

- Navigate to the Settings > Advanced features > Bixby Routines.

- Create routines like "When connected to Wi-Fi, enable Do Not Disturb" or "When charging, reduce screen brightness."

5. Pro Tips for Smooth Performance

Here are some expert tips to keep your Galaxy A16 running like new:

Clear Cache Regularly

Clearing cache data for apps can speed up your device by removing temporary files.

- Navigate to the Settings > Storage > Cached data and clear it periodically.

Use Adaptive Battery

Enable Adaptive Battery to limit battery usage by apps that you don't use often.

- Navigate to the Settings > Battery and device care > Battery > Adaptive Battery, and toggle it on.

Manage Notifications Effectively

Too many notifications can clutter your screen and drain battery life.

- Navigate to the Settings > Notifications > Do Not Disturb to set up quiet hours or silencing apps.

Enable Auto-Updates for Apps

Keep your apps updated automatically to get the latest features and security patches without needing to manually check for updates.

- Navigate to the Google Play Store > Menu (three lines) > Settings > Auto-update apps.

Quick Recap Table

Task	How to Do It	Tips
One-Handed Mode	Settings > Advanced features > One-handed mode	Swipe down diagonally from the bottom corners to activate
App Pair	Recent Apps > Select two apps > Tap App Pair	Use for multitasking in split-screen view
Battery-Saving Mode	Settings > Battery and device care > Battery > Power saving mode	Turn off background apps and use Dark mode
Google Assistant	Use voice commands like "Hey Google, set a reminder"	Control smart home devices and send texts hands-free
Bixby Routines	Settings > Advanced features > Bixby Routines	Automate tasks based on habits and locations
Clear Cache	Settings > Storage > Cached data > Clear	Regularly clear cache for better performance

Now that you've unlocked these hidden features, shortcuts, battery-saving hacks, and pro tips, you're ready to become a true Galaxy A16 expert! By mastering these advanced features, your phone will be faster, more efficient, and more enjoyable to use every day.